Mary-Kate & Ashley

OUR STORY

Mary-Kate & Ashley

OUR STORY

Mary-Kate & Ashley Olsen's
Official Biography

As told to Damon Romine

HarperEntertainment
An Imprint of HarperCollinsPublishers
A PARACHUTE PRESS BOOK

A PARACHUTE PRESS BOOK

Parachute Publishing, L.L.C.
156 Fifth Avenue
Suite 302
New York, NY 10010

Published by
HarperEntertainment
An Imprint of HarperCollins*Publishers*
10 East 53rd Street, New York, NY 10022-5299

Created and produced by
Parachute Press, L.L.C., in cooperation with Dualstar Publications, a division of Dualstar Entertainment Group, Inc., published by HarperEntertainment, an imprint of HarperCollins*Publishers*.

For information address HarperCollins Publishers Inc., 10 East 53rd Street, New York, NY 10022-5299.

ISBN 0-06-107569-8

HarperCollins®, ™ ® , and HarperEntertainment™ are trademarks of HarperCollins Publishers Inc.

First printing: January 2000

Printed in the United States of America

Visit HarperEntertainment on the World Wide Web at
www.harpercollins.com

10 9 8 7 6 5 4 3 2

Chapter 1

The Real Mary-Kate and Ashley

Maybe you think that Mary-Kate and Ashley are such big stars that you don't have a lot in common with them. But you and the girls are probably more alike than you think!

"We do everything other kids do," says Mary-Kate. "We go to school, shop with our friends, and have sleepovers."

"Our friends and teachers treat us just like regular kids," Ashley agrees.

The girls take trips to the mall, rush out to catch a new movie, and love seeing musicals. They used to take piano lessons but gave them up for soccer and cheerleading. They have crushes on celebrities—and guys at school. They listen to the music of

'N Sync and go to concerts with their friends.

Mary-Kate and Ashley were born on June 13, 1986. (Ashley is the older twin by two minutes!) They've grown up in suburban Los Angeles with their brother, Trent, who is two years older, and sister, Elizabeth, who is three years younger. Their parents are divorced, and the Olsen kids divide their time between living with their dad and with their mom. Their dad, Dave, is a mortgage broker. Their mom, Jarnette (Jarnie), used to dance with the Los Angeles Ballet.

"Trent is a typical big brother," Mary-Kate says. "He helps us with our homework. He likes to be our protector. But he also likes to tease us. He's great at drawing, and at sports, too. He plays soccer, baseball, and basketball. And he loves computer games!"

Lizzie, the younger sister, stands up for herself and is very independent. Right now, Lizzie is performing in school plays and really likes to act. She's starting to do professional work as an actress, too. She's already made her first commercial!

Mary-Kate and Ashley also have a new sister and brother from their dad's second marriage to McKenzie Olsen. Taylor is two and a half years old, and Jake is one and a half. "It's great having little kids to play with," Ashley says. "We help out with babysitting a lot. With so many kids around, the house gets really crazy sometimes. But we like it!"

"Our family is probably a lot like everyone else's," Mary-Kate says. "Sometimes we argue. You know how it goes: One minute everyone is watching TV. The next, a fight breaks out over the remote control. But most of the time, we get along great. We're very close and we stand up for each other. And we all share our stuff. But the rule is you have to ask before borrowing something!"

When all the kids were little, they played house together. Trent would play the dad. Lizzie always had to be the family pet.

But they could have used one of their real pets instead! Over the years, there have been plenty of animals in the Olsen household: Dogs, cats, birds, turtles, and hamsters. Now, the kids have a Teacup Yorkie named Lucy at their mom's house and two dogs at their dad's house. Mary-Kate also has two horses, CD and Star. She stables them at a nearby ranch.

Horseback riding is definitely Mary-Kate's favorite activity. "I love horseback riding. I'd go for a riding lesson every day if I could," she says. Recently, Mary-Kate won an overall first-place medal at a horse show. She competes in categories like grooming and jumping.

While Mary-Kate is riding, Ashley keeps busy with dance class and tennis lessons. Her love of dance is something she inherited from her mother. Together, the girls study kickboxing. For Ashley, it's great mental and physical exercise. "And it's good for self-defense, too," Mary-Kate adds.

Both girls have very close friends whom they see all the time. They each have their own special friends, of course, but they also have good friends in common. Mary-Kate and Ashley and their friends go Rollerblading, to the mall, to the beach, to Disneyland or to an amusement park called Knott's Berry Farm. "The best part is that we're finally tall enough to be able to go on all the rides," says Ashley. "We ride every roller coaster there is!"

Once the girls took all their friends to Magic Mountain to film a roller coaster scene for their video, *You're Invited to Mary-Kate & Ashley's Birthday Party*. To get the scene, the whole group had to ride the roller coaster eight times in a row! "We all got so dizzy we could hardly stand," Ashley remembers.

"Sometimes we hang out with our friends at our house," Mary-Kate says. "There's always something fun to do. Especially swimming! We have a pool in the backyard. Ashley and I learned to swim when we were very little—and we love it!"

The Real Mary-Kate and Ashley

The girls have had many awesome birthday parties in their backyard, too. Sometimes their parents hired disc jockeys to spin records and teach the girls new dances. They've also rented an inflatable Moonbounce for the kids to bounce in. Of course, there was always plenty of food and games—and swimming!

"Next to birthday parties, we love sleepovers with our friends," Mary-Kate says. "We love to stay up late. We dance and sing, watch videos, tell ghost stories, and make our own custom pizzas. We have a blast!"

Ashley and Mary-Kate have rooms at both their mom's and their dad's places. At their dad's, the rooms are down the hall from each other. Ashley's room is fully decorated. Mary-Kate has been so busy with her horses lately that she hasn't really done much with hers yet. But she's starting to pick furniture from a catalog.

Both girls have put up posters on their walls. They display lots of pictures, too, from their days on *Full House*, their travels, and their TV show *Two of a Kind*. They also have plenty of photos of their family.

Mary-Kate and Ashley each have their own stereo and TV in their bedroom. When asked about their favorite TV shows, they answer at the exact same time: "We like *Friends* and *Party of Five*!" They might add "late-night infomercials" to that list too—both girls admit to falling asleep with the TV on!

Mary-Kate and Ashley recently got new computers. They took a typing course in school, so they're getting faster and faster on their keyboards. And they've discovered the Internet. The girls can now research subjects on the World Wide Web for school. And, of course, their friends across the country are just a click away through e-mail. Ashley, especially, likes to keep in touch with her friends that she met from *Two of a Kind* through the computer.

The girls—and their parents—take school very, very seriously. Their parents make sure that Mary-Kate and Ashley are getting the best education possible. Even when the girls are working on a TV show or movie, they don't miss a day of class. The classroom just has to go where they go!

"A lot of people probably think that going on location must be cool because then we get to miss school," says Ashley. "Wrong!"

"The law says we have to spend a certain number of hours each day in school while we're working," Mary-Kate explains. "Besides, when we're done shooting and go back home, we don't want to be behind the rest of our class."

The Real Mary-Kate and Ashley

The girls keep up by having studio teachers right there on the set. The studio teachers give all the same homework and tests their regular teachers give. Usually, they have one teacher for language arts and social studies, and one for math and science.

The girls do well in all their school subjects. They particularly enjoy creative writing. They like to write short stories. Sometimes they also keep journals about the many places they've visited.

Ashley and Mary-Kate admit their studio teachers can get tough when necessary to make sure all their homework gets done. "Sometimes they'll crack the whip to make sure we finish on time," admits Mary-Kate. "But actually, *we* want to get it done and over with just as much as they do!"

When the girls are doing a TV show, the studio classroom looks just like a regular classroom—with desks, and computers, and maps on the wall. But when Mary-Kate and Ashley are traveling to make a movie, they use any room that is available. "We've had classrooms in trailers, in lobbies—once, even in a large closet!" Ashley remembers.

When the schoolwork is done, there's still time for school fun on the set. Mary-Kate and Ashley's studio classroom gets decorated for the holidays, just like regular school. The girls love Christmas! And they exchange cards with their studio friends on Valentine's Day.

The truth is, Mary-Kate and Ashley try to have as much fun as possible while they're working. That's not always easy. Sometimes people are a little nervous being around the girls at first. But it doesn't take long for them to realize that Mary-Kate and Ashley don't *act* famous. The girls do their best to make everyone feel really comfortable. They don't think they're better than anybody else just because they're in show business. And Mary-Kate and Ashley are the first to reach out and help others in need. "They're genuinely good, sweet, compassionate kids," the girls' studio teacher says.

What makes Mary-Kate and Ashley so, well— normal? They say they have their mom and dad to thank.

"The most important thing our parents have taught us is to respect other people," says Mary-Kate. "They teach us not to be like Hollywood stars and to be like normal kids. And we are."

Chapter 2

Being Twins Is Double the Fun!

"Is it fun being a twin?"

That's the number one question Mary-Kate and Ashley's fans ask.

And the answer is a huge "YES!"

Sisters are often very close. But twin sisters are built-in best friends! "We always have each other to talk with," Mary-Kate explains. "We share all our big secrets," adds Ashley.

Like most twins, Mary-Kate and Ashley share a special bond. Each of them often seems to know what the other is thinking—without saying a word. "Ashley can tell things about me, like if something is bothering me—or if I think a boy is cute!" Mary-Kate says.

The girls have a great time together. Mary-Kate is known to be more of a prankster, but both girls have a great sense of humor. In fact, Ashley usually jumps right in on Mary-Kate's practical jokes. But it's all in the name of fun. The girls' favorite prank is to clip a clothespin on the back of a friend's shirt. Then they wait—and giggle—to see how long it takes before their friend notices!

"Mary-Kate could be a bit sneaky when she was little," reveals her mom, Jarnie. "Once, when the twins were very young, money was missing from all the kids' piggy banks."

"And suddenly Mary-Kate was very wealthy," adds their dad, Dave. "We divided the money back up and returned it to the correct piggy banks. Then Mary-Kate was benched for a while."

Being a twin isn't just fun. There are other benefits, too. Think about how practical it would be to have someone who looks exactly like you. When the girls go shopping together, they choose different clothes to take in the dressing room. Who needs a mirror when you can see how an outfit looks on your twin?

Of course, everyone always expects twins to trade places with each other. You've seen it on TV shows, where a twin switches places to take a test in school. Or to go out on a date. Or to fool a friend. In one episode of Mary-Kate and Ashley's most recent TV series, *Two of a Kind*, the girls switched places to fool their dad. They did it again in their TV movie *Switching Goals* and in their feature film, *It Takes Two*. In real life, though, Mary-Kate and Ashley swear they haven't fooled their parents on purpose that way. "We haven't tried it yet," Ashley says with a grin.

Or maybe they just don't remember. "They did try some switcheroos around age five," their mom says. "But ultimately they can't fool me or their dad."

Well, most of the time, anyway. Once, when the twins were shooting their *Ballet Party* video, their dad called out, "Ashley, come here. I want to ask you something." But he was really talking to Mary-Kate! The whole film crew laughed. Their dad's mistake probably made the crew feel better about all the times *they'd* gotten the girls mixed up.

Still, it isn't always easy to guess who's who. Everyone seems to come up with a different way to tell Mary-Kate and Ashley apart. The girls' TV dad on *Full House*, Bob Saget, used to have problems. "When I got them mixed up," he once said, "I would get the hands-on-the-hips and the `Don't-you-know-

Mary-Kate and Ashley were born on June 13, under the sign of Gemini. It makes sense—Gemini is the sign of twins! Geminis often have great communication skills, just like Mary-Kate and Ashley. They are fun-loving, outgoing, and quick-minded. Geminis can also adapt easily to new situations. And best of all, just like Mary-Kate and Ashley, Geminis love people—especially their friends!

me-by-now?' attitude. When their personalities came out more, I started being able to tell them apart."

Sometimes, when the girls are getting their hair cut, their hairstylist gets them confused. He'll forget whose hair he started cutting and have to ask, "Which one are you again?"

But Mary-Kate and Ashley don't get mad when people mistake them for each other. They're used to it. They just smile and say, "My name is Ashley (or Mary-Kate), not Mary-Kate (or Ashley)!"

Even though the girls look so much alike, they are not identical twins! Mary-Kate and Ashley are fraternal twins. Fraternal twins sometimes look similar to each other, but they are not exactly the same.

There *are* ways to tell Mary-Kate and Ashley

apart. As infants, their parents used their freckles to figure out who was whom. Now, at thirteen, Ashley is slightly taller. Mary-Kate's face is a bit rounder. Ashley is right-handed, while Mary-Kate is left-handed.

"I think we looked more alike when we were younger, but not now," Ashley says.

"I'm the cute one," jokes Mary-Kate. "Just kidding."

For work, the girls have often had to look as similar as possible—especially during their time on *Full House*, when they played the same part. But as Mary-Kate and Ashley get older, they've each been experimenting with different looks.

When their *Two of a Kind* TV show came to an end, the girls decided to change their hairstyle. Mary-Kate cut her hair shorter, since she's so active and sporty. It was cute and it looked great on Mary-Kate. For a while, she clearly had her own look.

But there was just one glitch: Ashley loved Mary-Kate's short hair—and she wanted her own hair cut the same way. Before they knew it, the girls looked alike again. And then Mary-Kate decided to go even shorter! Today Mary-Kate's hair is shorter and more layered than Ashley's.

DID YOU KNOW?

• Spring is the time of the year that most twins are born (just like Mary-Kate and Ashley, who were born in June).

• More than half of all twins are born male.

• More twins are left-handed, like Mary-Kate, than are people who are not twins.

• Fraternal twins, like Mary-Kate and Ashley, are more likely to run in the family than are identical twins.

• Female fraternal twins and their sisters are more likely to give birth to twins.

The clothes department is another area where Mary-Kate and Ashley have similar tastes. Sometimes they buy the same outfits or accessories, but each girl picks a different color so they never end up dressing alike.

There's another reason Mary-Kate and Ashley don't dress alike. Mary-Kate rides horses and plays sports, so she often just pulls her hair into a ponytail and throws on jeans and a T-shirt. Ashley, on the other hand, enjoys experimenting with makeup and putting outfits together. "She sometimes dresses a little more fancy than I do and wears more skirts and dresses," Mary-Kate says with a shrug.

Being Twins Is Double the Fun!

As they get older, both girls are getting more into fashion and style—and sometimes one girl wants what the other one has. "When Mary-Kate and Ashley want to wear the same outfit, it gets a little crazy," their dad says with a laugh. This happened once when the girls were getting dressed for a Spice Girls concert. They both wanted to wear the same brown jacket with their black pants. This time, Mary-Kate won—and she got to wear it. (Ashley wore a blue jacket.) The next time, Ashley got to pick first. The girls have also been known to argue over who has the cooler, more grown-up shoes.

So, how do the girls work out their occasional differences? "We talk it over, and then we usually decide to take turns," Ashley explains. "Mary-Kate will wear something one time and I'll wear it the next time."

In fact, the girls don't compete with each other at all. They look out for each other, and give each other advice. And when they're acting, they always help each other out. For instance, during the filming of their recent movie *Passport to Paris*, Mary-Kate had to give a speech about Notre Dame cathedral. It included big words like "flying buttresses" (an architectural term)—and Mary-Kate kept tripping up on the words! Ashley gently touched her shoulder and said, "Don't worry, you'll get it." Later, when Ashley had an even longer speech, Mary-Kate was able to encourage *her*.

The girls make a terrific team because they are so supportive of each other. Sure, they can get on each other's nerves. All sisters do. They have sibling squabbles just like any family. But in the end, Ashley and Mary-Kate are always best friends.

Chapter 3

The *Full House* Years

How did Mary-Kate and Ashley get started in show business?

It all began when the girls were just seven months old. Their mom took them to a modeling agency. Mary-Kate and Ashley were beautiful babies. And the fact that they were twins was a bonus. The modeling agency quickly signed up both girls and lined up auditions.

But Jarnie didn't expect that they would actually get work. "I just thought it might be fun," she admits. "It was a way to get out of the house and do something a little out-of-the-ordinary."

Then Jarnie took the girls to a TV audition with executive producer Bob Boyett. Mr. Boyett was looking for young twins to play baby Michelle on a new ABC comedy. The show was called *Full House*.

When kids are working on a movie or television series, the law says they can only work for a few hours each day. Hiring twins means you are able to split the work between them.

By the time Mary-Kate and Ashley had their audition, there was already another set of twins in place to play the part of baby Michelle. But Mr. Boyett changed his mind when he met the Olsens. "I just thought they were so unique," he says. "They had these big expressive eyes. They were friendly and they listened when you spoke to them. And they would really respond to you!"

Plus, the girls looked a lot like the two big sisters on the TV show. Candace Cameron had been hired to play D.J., and Jodie Sweetin would play middle sister Stephanie.

Mary-Kate and Ashley were perfect for *Full House*! The fact that they were fraternal—not identical—twins could have been a problem, though. As babies, the girls looked almost exactly alike, so they could both be Michelle. But what would happen as the girls grew up? Would they still look alike?

Maybe you've seen the classic TV show *Bewitched* on Nickelodeon. On that show, twins were hired to play the role of baby Tabitha. But when they got older, their looks changed enough that you could tell them apart! Eventually one twin was chosen to continue playing the part.

Would the same thing happen with Mary-Kate and Ashley? Nobody knew!

Full House was a comedy about a different kind of family: Three grown men raising three little girls. Danny Tanner, played by actor Bob Saget, was the dad. Danny had just lost his wife in a car accident and was left to raise his three daughters, D.J., Stephanie, and Michelle, by himself. But he needed help. So his best friend Joey (played by comic Dave Coulier) and brother-in-law Jesse (actor John Stamos) moved in to help out.

The three men didn't have very much in common. Danny was a television announcer, Joey was a stand-up comic and part-time inventor, and Jesse wanted to be a rock-and-roll singer. There was always something crazy going on in that household!

By the time the show began in September 1987, Ashley and Mary-Kate were already a year old. Most of their first scenes involved Michelle just being a baby. Uncle Joey would make a mess changing her diaper. Uncle Jesse would sing her a lullaby. Michelle would try to take a few steps.

Mary-Kate & Ashley: Our Story

As the producers worked more and more with Mary-Kate and Ashley, they saw what special talents each of them could bring to the show. Although they looked alike, each twin had a distinct personality. "The girls could play so many different emotions because Ashley and Mary-Kate were so different," says their mom.

Once the producers realized that, it was easy to decide which twin would play which scene. In the early years, baby Ashley handled the sensitive scenes. Mary-Kate got the scenes where Michelle needed to be tough and sassy. As the girls' personalities developed, so did their roles. "Ashley became more serious and she was given all the serious lines," says their mom. "When they needed someone to be more active or emotional, they let Mary-Kate do it."

DID YOU KNOW?
- The Tanner address is 1882 Gerard Street.
- All of the Tanner kids attended Frasier Street Elementary School.
- Michelle's birthday is in November.
- Jesse's last name was Cochran, but in the fourth season he changed it to his family's Greek name, Katsopolis.

As infants, the girls sometimes needed acting help. A cookie was often held in front of them so they would smile or giggle for the camera. And the girls' funny reactions helped make the show popular. When Mary-Kate and Ashley could finally speak, they learned their lines by mimicking their acting coach. The girls really impressed their coach because they were always willing to try something new. And they never said no to her. When they were old enough to read, they memorized their lines just like the other actors.

Baby Michelle was a hit! People were saying there was something special about *Full House*. Never before had a show dared to give a baby such a big part, week after week. But this time Mary-Kate and Ashley made it possible.

More and more people tuned in to see the show—and the amazing Michelle Tanner. And after a couple of seasons, *Full House* became one of the top ten shows on television!

"I think it was the first time anyone really had a chance to watch a baby grow up on television," says the girls' mom. "They captured the audience's hearts."

Viewers were thrilled that Michelle was played by twins. The show played up the fact by having

Mary-Kate and Ashley appear opposite each other. Two Michelles would sometimes appear together in a dream. Once, Michelle even met her look-alike cousin from Greece.

The girls were unaware of all the excitement around them. They never realized how popular they were. Every day, Mary-Kate and Ashley just looked forward to going to the Warner Bros. Studios lot in Burbank, California, to see their "family" of co-workers. "The lot and the set were like a second home to us," says Mary-Kate.

The girls had fun playing with their young co-stars and with the golden retriever who played Comet. Jodie Sweetin and some of the kid guest stars would often visit Mary-Kate and Ashley in their dressing room. The girls got to decorate the room the way they wanted. It was full of games and art supplies. They often watched videos of classic musicals such as *Oklahoma*, *Guys and Dolls*, *My Fair Lady*, and *West Side Story*. No wonder that Ashley and Mary-Kate went on to star in so many musical videos of their own.

Going to the studio was a comfortable experience for them. "We grew up around all the people on *Full House*," says Mary-Kate. "That's what made it so much fun for us to go to work every day. We didn't do it because we had to. We did it because we loved it." The girls even complained about not working on Saturdays.

As the girls got older, the show began featuring episodes that mirrored what was really happening in their lives: Starting kindergarten. Learning to read. Riding a bicycle for the first time. Playing soccer. Dancing. Even Mary-Kate's love of horses was written into the story when Michelle took up riding.

DID YOU KNOW?
- The Tanners' phone number is 555-2424.
- D.J.'s private phone number is 555-8722.
- Michelle's middle name is Elizabeth.
- Tahj Mowry, who played Michelle's friend Teddy, is the younger brother of twins Tia and Tamera Mowry from *Sister Sister*.

As the series continued, the girls' talent shined even brighter. "We were delighted," says their producer. "As they grew up, they were learning from very talented comedians on the show. And they began acting on their own very early. The girls weren't having lines fed to them. They were studying acting and taking classes and becoming very good actresses."

Mary-Kate & Ashley: Our Story

Mary-Kate and Ashley don't have much time these days to watch television. But sometimes they'll watch an old rerun of *Full House*. The girls are their own toughest critics. "Sometimes we look at what we did back then and think we could have done it better," admits Mary-Kate. *Full House* fans may not agree.

After eight years, the show finally came to an end in 1995. But eight years is a great success in television. In fact, *Full House* is one of ABC's longest running comedies ever!

There's an extra bonus for Mary-Kate and Ashley and their family. They have an incredible video collection of the twins growing up, and they didn't even have to break out their own video camera!

Mary-Kate and Ashley still miss working on *Full House*. They especially miss their TV family. "It's sad not to see everyone we grew up with," says Mary-Kate.

The girls are in touch with the *Full House* bunch on a regular basis. They all get together for special events. Ashley and Mary-Kate attended baby showers for their co-stars Candace Cameron Bure (D.J.) and Lori Loughlin (Rebecca). And they were also at the wedding of John Stamos (Uncle Jesse), who married supermodel Rebecca Romijn. Seeing their

friends is always fun, but the girls admit it sometimes makes them even more "homesick" for their
Full House days.

But after the super-successful show ended, many
exciting new opportunities were in store for Mary-
Kate and Ashley. Their adventure was just begin-
ning!

Chapter 4

Movies! Movies! Movies!

Because of the huge popularity of *Full House*, people couldn't get enough of Mary-Kate and Ashley. A talking Michelle doll even became a big hit in 1992. Maybe it was time for fans to see *both* of the girls acting at the same time.

So that's what they did! Mary-Kate and Ashley each had their own part to play in their first television movie. The movie was called *To Grandmother's House We Go*. The girls made it during their summer break in 1992. When it aired on TV a few months later, it was one of the most-watched movies of the season.

Mary-Kate fell in love with her co-star in the movie: a miniature pony named Four-by-Four. For months afterward, when asked if she liked any boys in her school, the six-year-old would merely grin and say, "I have a crush on Four-by-Four." One day, Mary-Kate's dad even found her packing to go and visit the horse. Unfortunately, the pony lived in Vancouver, Canada—far away from the girls' home in Los Angeles.

To Grandmother's House We Go was a turning point for Ashley and Mary-Kate. The movie showed everyone that the girls were an important Hollywood team—not just as the TV character Michelle Tanner. Together, they would go on to make films, home videos, television specials, interactive games, fashion dolls and accessories, music albums, and even a series of books based on their twin characters. And they were still just kids! Whew!

Mary-Kate and Ashley's first album, *Brother for Sale*, was a hit, too. "My favorite song is `Brother for Sale'," Mary-Kate said after the album was finished. The girls may have gotten some ideas for that song from their older brother, Trent. "When we were rehearsing it, Trent said, `I hate that song!'" recalls Ashley. "But we love our brother," Mary-Kate is quick to point out.

In 1993, the girls released their first music video,

called simply, *Our First Video*. It featured a collection of songs from the girls' first two albums, *Brother for Sale* and *I Am the Cute One*. Mary-Kate and Ashley worked with a dance teacher to learn routines for the songs. But a lot of what ended up in the final video was the girls just having a blast, jumping around and bouncing on the bed!

One of their favorite songs from that video is *No One Tells the President What to Do*. "The song is about grown-ups telling you what to do all the time," Ashley explains. "But the president is lucky because nobody bosses him around. You can bet no one tells him to clean his room or eat his vegetables!"

Our First Video was another big success for Ashley and Mary-Kate. To celebrate, they took eight of their friends to a restaurant for all the hamburgers and milkshakes they wanted—and they went in a limo!

Even though Mary-Kate and Ashley made quite a splash with their music, they still wanted to act. Their second TV movie for ABC was also shot in Canada. It was the spooky Halloween film, *Double, Double, Toil and Trouble*. The girls had a great time making that movie because of all the crazy costumes they wore and the fun things that happened in the story.

Movies! Movies! Movies!

1994 was a big year for Mary-Kate and Ashley. The two made an appearance in the film *The Little Rascals*. The girls show up in a slumber party scene. Rent it and see if you can spot them!

The girls also returned to Canada to film the TV movie, *How the West Was Fun*. Mary-Kate was especially thrilled because she got to ride a horse again.

But the big news from Mary-Kate and Ashley that year was the grand opening of the Olsen and Olsen Mystery Agency. They got to play detectives in *The Adventures of Mary-Kate & Ashley*, a new series of detective videos. Nicknamed "The Trenchcoat Twins," the two adopted the motto "Will Solve Any Crime by Dinner Time." They were helped by their basset hound sidekick, Clue. The girls investigated all kinds of mysteries: in a spooky amusement park, aboard a U.S. Navy destroyer, at Sea World of Florida, at Waikiki Beach, Hawaii, at a volcano, and at many other exciting places. "We have *so* much fun," Ashley says. "It's like playing all the time."

Imagine riding horses and roller coasters, pretending to be rock stars, and taking fantastic cruises—all as part of your job!

The girls' fans loved the *Adventures of Mary-Kate & Ashley* videos so much that a series of books based on the videos soon followed. Next came *The New Adventures of Mary-Kate & Ashley* books, all-new, original mysteries for the Trenchcoat Twins to solve. The girls are involved in the writing of each book. "We meet with the editors and tell them things we like to do," says Mary-Kate. "I like to horseback ride, so there was a horseback riding adventure. We both like to surf, so there's a surfing book. And Ashley likes ballet, so we did a ballet story."

Mary-Kate and Ashley's videos are created the same way the books are created. The girls' real lives are turned into fun, musical stories. That's how their second series of videos, *You're Invited to Mary-Kate & Ashley's*, came about. The girls love to throw parties for their friends. By making these videos, they could share the fun with their fans and friends at home.

The girls began with one of their favorites, *Sleepover Party*, and then the parties started getting bigger. The girls learned how to surf for their *Hawaiian Beach Party* and how to ski for their *Christmas Party*.

In 1995, something really big happened to Mary-Kate and Ashley. They got to star in their very first feature film! That meant you could go see the movie at your neighborhood theater instead of on TV. In *It*

Takes Two, the girls played identical orphans, one rich and one poor, who had never met. When they

---

HOW MOVIES ARE MADE

LIGHTS

When you make a movie or video you need lots of lights. It's like using a flash to make the film in your camera work. Even a night scene has to be well-lit! It can get very hot working under so many lights. A makeup artist is always standing by in case makeup starts to melt. Lighting is very important in making a scene look interesting, bright, and colorful.

CAMERA

Of course, you need a camera to make a film. Mary-Kate and Ashley use several cameras when making their movies. There is always a close-up camera on each of the girls. Another camera films the whole scene, which is called a wide shot.

ACTION

That's what the director says when he's ready for the girls to start acting. When you see a film or video, you may see only the actors. But there are many other people on the other side of the camera. All of them are needed to make a movie. They include the director, assistant director, production designer, art director, camera operators, sound and lighting technicians, and people to handle hair, makeup, and wardrobe.

---

discover each other, they come up with a scheme to make their guardians fall in love.

For Mary-Kate and Ashley, the best thing about making videos and movies is that they get to travel to really exciting places. One of their family's favorite vacation spots is Hawaii. So guess what? In 1996, the entire family got to have a surf-and-sun vacation while Mary-Kate and Ashley made four videos in Hawaii! The girls played in the sand for *You're Invited to Mary-Kate & Ashley's Hawaiian Beach Party*. They got to raid the mini-refrigerator in their Hawaiian hotel room for *The Case Of The Hotel Who-Done-It*. "That was the best part," recalls Mary-Kate. "Our refrigerator was stocked full of candy and soda—and we got to eat it *all* for the video! The fruit chews were the best! In real-life, anything you eat gets added to your hotel bill, but this time it was free!"

The two other videos the girls made in Hawaii were *The Case Of The Volcano Mystery* and *The Case Of The U.S. Navy Adventure*.

Even though she loved working in Hawaii, Ashley's favorite video is no surprise: *Ballet Party*, with the New York City Ballet! Finally, she had a chance to show off her dancing talent. "I got to live out one of my big dreams," says Ashley.

Mary-Kate had the upper hand for the girls' next

video. *Camp Out Party* was right in Mary-Kate's neck of the woods! Sleeping in a tent. Hiking in fresh air. Fishing and roasting marshmallows. "Not a few of my twin sister's favorite things," teases Mary-Kate, "but we managed to get Ashley there anyhow."

In 1998, Mary-Kate and Ashley made another movie called *Billboard Dad*. Again, Mary-Kate and Ashley got to do things they enjoy in real life. Mary-Kate played Tess, a surfer, and Ashley played Emily, a high diver. In the story, the girls teamed up to find a new love for their single dad—by placing an ad on a billboard!

A year later, the girls were back in front of the cameras for another big movie. This time around, Mary-Kate and Ashley were asked where they'd like to shoot it. They both said, "Europe!" Through all their travels, the girls had been dying to go there. *Passport to Paris* was written and the girls went off to France to film it.

In *Passport to Paris*, Mary-Kate played Melanie and Ashley played Allison, two girls who are sent to stay with their grandfather in Paris during spring break. Of course, it wouldn't be any fun if the girls didn't get into mischief while exploring the Eiffel Tower . . . or while riding around the city on motor scooters with cute boys!

After filming *Passport to Paris*, Mary-Kate and Ashley went on to Rome, Italy, with friends and family. They had a fabulous time shopping, eating, and sightseeing.

The girls like to make movies that are fun for them to do—and just as fun for *you* to watch. Before they start shooting, Ashley and Mary-Kate sit down with the script and read it aloud. They point out things like, "I would never say that," or "That's not really a cool name, let's pick another one." The girls work on the script until they agree it's exactly right.

As Mary-Kate and Ashley head into the new millenium, they have lots of new projects to look forward to. They've just finished their first CD-ROM, *Mary-Kate & Ashley's Dance Party of the Century*, and their first GameBoy Color, *The New Adventures of Mary-Kate & Ashley*, and will be releasing a new console video game soon. In addition, they are developing a state-of-the-art Internet site and a new line of Mary-Kate and Ashley fashions, cosmetics, and accessories featuring the hottest styles and trends, as well as more movies, TV specials, and TV shows. So be on the lookout for upcoming products and events. Whatever Mary-Kate and Ashley do next, it's sure to be fun!

Chapter 5

Behind the Scenes with Mary-Kate and Ashley

Want to know what *really* happens when Mary-Kate and Ashley go on location? The girls' real life is just as exciting—and funny—as the one you see on-screen! Here are some sneak peeks at what Mary-Kate and Ashley were up to when the cameras weren't rolling.

You already know Mary-Kate loves horses. Ashley's not quite the rider her sister is, so she's usually given a tamer horse. While in the Canadian Rockies filming *How the West Was Fun*, Ashley rode a horse named Winston. She called him "totally boring," until the day he took off in a gallop with seven-year-old Ashley holding tight! Real cowboys on the set took off to rescue her. But there was no need. When they finally brought Winston to a stop, Ashley giggled, "That was fun!"

The girls had all kinds of adventures in Canada. On the weekends, they went white water rafting. Were they scared of being thrown around the choppy, bouncing rapids? "Not a bit!" both girls said. At age seven, Mary-Kate and Ashley were also brave enough to walk across the entire Capilano Bridge. It's a long, narrow bridge that rocks back and forth more than 100 feet in the air. It's awesome!

The girls have also shot videos at Sea World in Orlando, Florida. They slipped into wetsuits and sat on the backs of killer whales Shamu and Namu. "They are *so* big and they look kind of scary," Ashley admits. The girls also rode dolphins and waddled with penguins.

While filming *The Case Of The Volcano Mystery*, Mary-Kate and Ashley felt like they were on a safari. "We had to hike about half a mile into the rainforest to get where we were shooting," remembers Ashley. "The trees were so tall and so thick you couldn't even see the sky over us." Not only was it dark, but it was very humid, too. The girls had to drink lots of water to keep from getting dehydrated.

Speaking of water, how many kids do you know

who get to sail out to sea on a real U.S. Navy destroyer? That's just what Mary-Kate and Ashley did in *The Case Of The U.S. Navy Adventure*! "In the video it looks like we actually led lots of other ships out to sea. But the truth was, the Navy was actually taking part in exercises at sea with ships from other countries," explains Mary-Kate. "We got to see ships from as far away as Japan!"

"The best part was when we were leaving the ship, we were all dressed up in full sailor outfits," says Ashley. "And we got piped off. That's when a sailor plays a tune on a little pipe when someone comes or goes off the ship."

To thank the sailors for all their help, Mary-Kate and Ashley visited the ship after it returned to Pearl Harbor. The crew brought their children on board to meet the girls. The day turned into a major party—on one of the most powerful military ships in the world!

Ashley and Mary-Kate had so much fun on the Navy destroyer they were eager for another awesome adventure. It turned out to be an out-of-this-world adventure on a space shuttle! It was for their next video, *The Case Of The U.S. Space Camp Mission*, and they actually attended the U.S. Space Camp in Huntsville, Alabama. "Trent, Dad, Ashley and I attended a weekend Parent-Child session," says Mary-Kate. "We were each given different assignments to plan and carry out on a pretend space shuttle mission. We also got to work at mission control, build and launch model rockets to 400 feet, and operate shuttle simulators. Trent loves video games, so he really went wild!"

The highlight of the girls' U.S. Space Camp experience was having dinner with a famous astronaut, Alan Bean. Mr. Bean was the fourth astronaut to walk on the moon, during the Apollo XII mission in 1970. (Apollo XII was the second spaceship to land on the moon.) "We felt so honored to have dinner with one of only twelve people on Earth who have ever touched the moon," says Ashley. The girls learned a lot about space from Mr. Bean. They asked him a ton of questions, like what it felt like to see the Earth from a space ship. "It was one of our best evenings ever," recalls Mary-Kate, "and he had a big part in our video, too."

For the video, the girls suited up as astronauts. Then they rode in space simulators, where they could experience how it would really feel to walk on the moon. Well, sort of walk and sort of float. On the moon there's not much gravity to hold you down!

Behind the Scenes with Mary-Kate and Ashley

Ashley and Mary-Kate also had one adventure no astronaut ever had to deal with! The nine-year-old girls were missing a couple of their front teeth after being visited by the Tooth Fairy. So the gaps wouldn't show on video or TV, they each used fake front teeth called "flippers." But when they left for U.S. Space Camp, they left their "teeth" on their bathroom counter back home. Mary-Kate and Ashley wound up running around Huntsville, Alabama looking for a dentist to make their emergency flippers. Luckily, they found someone to help them get their teeth in place just in time!

Compared to walking on the moon and finding new front teeth, learning to surf was easy. Professional surfer Brian Kealanu taught Mary-Kate and Ashley how to surf. "Even though we lived in California all our lives, we had never learned to surf," admits Mary-Kate. "It was great to have a surfing champion teach us. We were riding the waves in fifteen minutes!"

It's not much of a surprise that the girls are so quick to learn new skills. They're always ready and willing to try something different. And they're not afraid of taking chances. Mary-Kate and Ashley are always ready to jump in when the director yells "Action!"

Surfing wasn't the only water sport the girls

Mary-Kate and Ashley's Surfing Lingo

Wipeout: When you are thrown off the board into the ocean.

Over the falls: A wipeout when the wave crashes over you and you are thrown up over it, like going over a waterfall.

Tubed: Surfing inside the wave, under the curl.

Stoked: Feeling excited about the waves!

Floater: When you board up to the lip of the wave and float down while you ride the board.

Off the lip: When you are on the very top of the wave, you go through the edge of the wave and it forces you down.

Got the fever: Feeling like you have to go out and surf!

Courtesy of *Our Funzine*

enjoyed in Hawaii. "Once we got to go on jet skis," Ashley remembers. "They were a blast. We wanted to drive them ourselves, but you have to be over 18, so Mary-Kate and I rode with adults. It was still cool when we raced each other and jumped through waves like dolphins. Awesome!"

For the girls' *Christmas Party* video in 1997, they headed to Vail, Colorado. There was no snow back home in Los Angeles, so Mary-Kate and Ashley were thrilled to have a white Christmas. The girls had played around on snow skis before during family vacations. But now they were going to be on video—and they had to look like expert skiers!

"A few extra lessons never hurt," quips Mary-Kate. "In Vail, our teachers were Erick, John, and Sarah. They were great! By the middle of the day, we were whipping down the slopes and hopping over bumps. We could even stop at the end of the run without falling down—most of the time, anyway!"

For the video, a cameraman skied ahead of the twins—going backward! "We had a hard enough time going forward," says Ashley. "Can you imagine how hard it would be to ski backward?" The girls got plenty of chances to perfect their skiing during the shoot. If the director didn't like the take, they hopped back on the chair lift and skied down the hill. Again. And again. And again.

The girls had a ball in the snow. Besides skiing, they also got to go snow tubing, bobsledding ("That was kind of scary," says Ashley), and snowmobiling.

"Vail was so amazing," Mary-Kate said afterward. "Next time we'll have to bring Trent and Lizzie and show them our new moves!"

The girls came in from the cold for their *Ballet Party* video with the New York City Ballet. "We had to practice with our choreographer for days before the actual shoot," Ashley says. "Because I've taken dance lessons for so long, I had a pretty good idea of what the steps were. But you should have seen Mary-Kate!"

Mary-Kate admits she was a bit nervous about getting up on the stage. But she held her own. Ashley says, "Whether you're a dancer or an athlete, you have to have a lot of strength and coordination. Well, Mary-Kate had both. She worked really hard at all those plies and jetes, and she was great. I think she surprised everyone, especially herself," Ashley adds proudly.

When the girls went to France to film *Passport to Paris*, they didn't have to learn any special stunts or sports. But they still found new things to try.

Ashley was supposed to speak some French in the movie. So when the girls got to Paris, they both decided to speak the language whenever they could. Their French tutor travelled with them and they experimented on their own. They did their best to order in French while dining out. Once they were even daring enough to try escargot—snails! Snails are a delicacy in France. Ashley thought they were "trés bon," while Mary-Kate made it clear in English that she didn't care for the dish: "Yuck!"

But the big adventure for Ashley and Mary-Kate came in the boy department. *Passport to Paris* was the girls' first romantic comedy. At 13, they were each going to have their first screen kiss—and they would have to pull it off with a crew of 50 people standing around watching! Talk about pressure! The girls admit they were a little shy about having their first kiss in front of an audience. But they got plenty of chances to practice: They had to do it several times to get it just right for the camera!

Whether it's dancing on their toes, riding a killer whale at Sea World, or kissing a boy in Paris, Mary-Kate and Ashley are willing to give anything a try. And there's always a new adventure ahead for them.

Chapter 6

Two of a Kind

The three years after *Full House* ended were busy ones for Mary-Kate and Ashley. They loved working on their many film and video projects. And then in 1998, the girls got a chance to star together in a new ABC TV series, *Two of a Kind*.

The show was about twin girls named Mary-Kate and Ashley! But instead of Olsen, their last name was Burke. "Our characters were opposites," Mary-Kate says. "The producers took some of our own personality differences and exaggerated them. I played a tomboy whose biggest interest is perfecting her curveball. Ashley played a straight-A student who is starting to become interested in boys."

"I'm not as girlie in real life as I was on the

OUR FAMILY ALBUM

Here's a picture of us as babies. Admit it—we were pretty cute!

Luckily, our hair grew a little longer over the next few years! This picture shows us when we were five.

Here's a picture of us with our dad Dave, sister Lizzie, and brother Trent. Can you tell which twin is which?

This is us with our mom. She's the best!

We love Christmas! Here we are unwrapping two of our favorite presents—a model horse for Mary-Kate and an ice-cream maker for Ashley!

We love making books and videos. It's so much fun!

In 1997, we won the national first-place award for Best Children's Video Series for *The Adventures of Mary-Kate & Ashley*. How exciting is that?

We love getting dressed up—especially for Halloween.
When we were ten years old, we dressed up
as Raggedy Ann and Andy.

Our mom came to U.S. Space Camp with us.
We had a blast!

Here are Lizzie, Jake, Trent, Taylor, and Ashley celebrating after Lizzie's dance recital. Doesn't Lizzie's stage makeup look fabulous?

Here we are on our 1999 Alaska cruise with our stepmom, McKenzie, and sister Taylor. Isn't the scenery spectacular?

Being a twin means having a double birthday cake! This is when we turned nine.

One of the great things about being stars is getting to go to cool events like a Spice Girls concert. Here we are, all dressed up and ready to party!

show," Ashley says. And Mary-Kate agrees, "I'm not as sporty or tomboyish as my character. I still go to the mall and we both like shopping."

The make-believe Burke family lived in Chicago with their single dad, a college professor. He was on the hunt for a babysitter to watch the girls after school and be a good role model.

Actor Christopher Seiber played Mary-Kate and Ashley's dad. The babysitter was played by Sally Wheeler. This was Chris and Sally's big television break. They would be working with seasoned pros Mary-Kate and Ashley, who had already been in show business for 12 years.

"On the first day, I was terribly nervous," admits Sally. "I went up to the girls and said, `Well, you guys, you know I've never actually done something like this. I'm so nervous.' And they said, `Hey, don't worry. You can always do the scene again if you mess up. Come on, calm down.' Mary-Kate and Ashley were so generous and helpful."

Sally found that she actually had a lot in common with Mary-Kate and Ashley. Like Mary-Kate, Sally had a passion for horses. And like both girls, Sally enjoyed Rollerblading. The three of them could often be found taking a break, skating around the Warner Bros. Studios lot.

After the first episode, or "pilot," was completed, Mary-Kate spoke up. She wanted her character to have a softer look. "She really looked like a tomboy," Mary-Kate said. "They kept bringing me out in a football or basketball uniform. I didn't really like that, so we changed it. My character was still a tomboy who liked to hang out with all the guys. She loved to play football and basketball, but the way she dressed was a little different." Instead of sports jerseys, Mary-Kate got to wear jeans on the show. Ashley usually wore a dressier outfit. "That's definitely her style in real life," says Mary-Kate.

Mary-Kate and Ashley felt right at home on this show. For one thing, they were working with the same crew they worked with on *Full House*. Plus, both shows dealt with a single dad trying to raise his daughters. Both shows even featured a similar set: a living room with stairs to the left; a kitchen with a backdoor to the right. "The whole thing brought back memories of being on *Full House*," says Mary-Kate.

Once again, the girls had to divide their day between work and school. They worked five days a week. Every morning they studied with their studio teachers for three hours. Their schoolwork at the studio matched the work their classmates were doing back at Mary-Kate and Ashley's regular school.

The girls' studio classroom was in between their dressing rooms. On *Full House*, Mary-Kate and Ashley had shared a dressing room filled with toys and games. Now the girls had a chance to be creative with their own personal dressing rooms.

"We decorated our dressing rooms twice," reveals Mary-Kate. "The first time, mine was painted yellow with butterflies. Then we changed it to white. Ashley's room was white with butterflies. We changed hers to all white, too." Even though each girl had her own room, they found themselves hanging out in Mary-Kate's dressing room between takes.

When *Two of a Kind* first aired on TV in September, kids couldn't wait to see Mary-Kate and Ashley. The girls didn't disappoint their fans—they were fantastic in their new TV roles.

Two of a Kind only lasted for one season in its first run, though it continues every weekday on Fox Family Channel in reruns. Mary-Kate and Ashley still keep in touch with their co-stars Chris and Sally. They all try to get together whenever possible.

Even though their new show came to an end,

Mary-Kate & Ashley: Our Story

Mary-Kate and Ashley continue in television. More television specials will air soon, a primetime series is in the works, and an animated series is even being developed based on the Trenchcoat Twins. Keep your eyes peeled for the next time they pop up on TV!

Chapter 7

Mary-Kate and Ashley Ahoy!

Where would you go if you wanted to travel to new places, eat great food, dance until late in the evening, swim in the ocean—and best of all, spend a week with new friends? Aboard a cruise ship with Mary-Kate and Ashley, of course! The girls love to take fantastic floating vacations—and have fun with their fans at the same time!

It's incredible. The girls are only 13 years old and already they've been on *four* cruises! They took their first cruise when they were eight, on a Carnival Cruise ship called the *Sensation*. The girls couldn't believe it—the ship had two swimming pools, a game room and video arcade, and even a disco!

The ship left from Florida in December 1994 on a

week-long trip to the Caribbean, filled with fans eager to meet the Olsens. But Mary-Kate and Ashley's guests were in for another treat. They would appear in the background of the girls' new video, *The Case Of The Mystery Cruise*!

After Mary-Kate and Ashley finished work each day, they got to hang out with the other kids on the ship. The fun began with a scavenger hunt. Later the kids played games like Win, Lose or Draw, and Bingo. The girls also judged a Mummy Wrap contest and a talent show.

In the evenings, there was always a theme dinner, like "Formal Night" or "Disco Night" where everyone got to dress up. On "Island Night," Mary-Kate and Ashley wore colorful tropical dresses they had bought in Hawaii. After dinner, they did the limbo with all their new friends. When they went to bed that night, the girls agreed they'd had the best time ever. But something was bothering them.

Another night was "Country Western Night." The girls dressed like cowgirls. "And we got to show off some of our dance moves that we learned when we were in Calgary filming *How the West Was Fun*," recalls Ashley.

That night was a blast, too. But something was still bothering them.

Mary-Kate and Ashley Ahoy!

During the fun-filled week, the ship made stops in Cozumel and Playa del Carmen, Mexico. Mary-Kate and Ashley even got to swim with stingrays!

But the eight-year-old girls were still worried. The ship would return to Florida on Christmas morning. Would Santa be able to find them if they weren't home in Los Angeles?

"Mary-Kate didn't think so and I wasn't very sure myself," says Ashley. "But Dad kept insisting that there wasn't going to be any problem. He told us Santa Claus was a pretty magical kind of guy."

On Christmas Eve, everyone on board the ship said good-bye. "We were all taking lots of pictures to remember everything," says Ashley. "We couldn't wait to show them to our friends back home."

The night ended with a special dance party. Then it was off to bed to get a good night's sleep and wait for Santa.

On Christmas morning, Mary-Kate and Ashley woke up in their cabins to find that Santa hadn't come! He hadn't found them on the ocean after all!

"We were so disappointed," Mary-Kate says. "Dad calmed us down and explained that Santa probably left our toys at the hotel. That way we wouldn't have to pack them all up as soon as we opened them."

Ashley nods. "When we got off the ship and went back to the hotel there was a tree with lights and decorations and all kinds of presents. It was the coolest!"

But the largest gift couldn't be wrapped. "The best present of all was waiting for us back home in Los Angeles. It was a horse named CD for the whole family," says Ashley. "Mary-Kate was the most excited. She could hardly wait to get home and ride!"

The next year, the girls were back sailing on the Caribbean with their fans. This time they were aboard a different Carnival Cruise Line ship, the *Imagination*. And this time the girls didn't make any videos or television shows. "We spent the whole time making new friends, relaxing, and just having fun!" says Ashley.

"One of the best things was that some fans from the year before came back to take another vacation with us!" Mary-Kate adds.

And, as an added bonus, the family would be home in plenty of time for Christmas. Santa was definitely able to find them in 1995!

Because Mary-Kate and Ashley love to swim in

their backyard pool at home, they gave the ship's pool a try. "Ashley dove in and discovered that the pool was filled with salt water!" laughs Mary-Kate. "Boy, was she surprised! After that, we were all careful to keep our eyes shut and our mouths closed. The salt water didn't keep any of us from having fun, though. We played Marco Polo, Shark-Minnow, and a bunch of other water games."

The *Imagination* stopped at a place called Duns River Falls. There, Mary-Kate and Ashley and their friends climbed 1,500 feet up a narrow path to stand inside a waterfall. "It was so cool," Ashley says. "Definitely worth the hike!" Trent went into town and bought a drum at an outdoor bazaar. "We got to listen to that drum for the rest of our trip," recalls Mary-Kate with a shudder. "We really wanted to try to hide it. But we couldn't get it away from him!"

On the last day of the cruise, there was a big talent show. Some kids sang. Some danced. Others read poetry. Even Mary-Kate and Ashley got into the act. "We did a little skit with Lizzie and some friends. Everybody laughed a lot and had a good time," says Mary-Kate.

In August 1998, the girls returned to Florida for still another ship adventure. This time, they sailed aboard *Disney Magic*, the Disney Cruise Line ship.

About 200 families joined Mary-Kate and Ashley for four days at Disney World and four more days on the ship. What a blast!

"The first day we had a dance party at Planet Hollywood," says Ashley. "The place was rocking! They videotaped everyone and broadcast it on big screens all around the restaurant."

When it was time to board the *Disney Magic*, the dancing went on. Mary-Kate and Ashley hosted a bon voyage party next to the Goofy Pool. They danced with all their new friends as the ship pulled out of the harbor, embarking on a magical four-day cruise.

When the music wasn't blaring, there was snorkeling, paddleboats, and all the food the passengers could eat. But even taking a break in the cabins was fun. "Every single room was based on a different Disney story or theme," says Ashley. "And there were a whole bunch of antiques that made the rooms look really pretty," adds Mary-Kate.

Their suite was decorated in 1930s Art Deco style, with three bedrooms and a piano in the living room. "It was so big," recalls Mary-Kate. "We had seven television sets and could never decide which one to watch." The suite was compliments of the Los Angeles-based Sail with the Stars, the company that sponsored the cruise.

Mary-Kate and Ashley Ahoy!

Disney Magic docked at Castaway Cay, its very own private island. "It was like *Gilligan's Island*," Ashley says.

The girls ended the decade with one more fan cruise. In August 1999, they invited their fans on a completely different journey. This time the cruise went to Alaska!

Mary-Kate and Ashley danced seven fun-filled nights away and partied with a group of both new and old friends aboard the beautiful Holland America ship, the MS. *Veendam*. "It was named Ship of the Year in 1997, so we figured it'd be great," Mary-Kate says. "But it was amazing! It had the best disco ever!"

The girls had wanted this trip to be extra-special. It was their last summer vacation before starting the eighth grade and they wanted to celebrate. The ship set sail from Vancouver, Canada. During the 1,000-mile trip to Alaska's gold rush country, Mary-Kate and Ashley took part in rap sessions, fashion shows and, of course, dance parties!

But the real fun began when the ship arrived in Alaska. Mary-Kate and Ashley rode a float plane that landed on the water. And they hiked through the Alaskan wilderness. Even though it was August, all the mountains were still cold and snow-covered.

They saw enormous glaciers and even avalanches. They also went on a treasure hunt and took a hayride with their fans. The girls kayaked in the ocean and went horseback riding. That made Mary-Kate, who was missing her two horses back home, happiest of all.

"It was a great way to unwind before school started," says Ashley, with a sigh. "Cruises are the best, because you're not staying in the same place all the time. You're out in the ocean in the middle of nowhere with a whole bunch of friends."

In June 2000, Mary-Kate and Ashley will be traveling to Russia and Scandinavia on a new super Sail with the Stars cruise event called To Russia With Love. The ship will visit Helsinki, Finland; Stockholm, Sweden; Moscow and St. Petersburg, Russia; and other places as well. And after that— who knows? But maybe next time *you'll* be hitting the high seas with Mary-Kate and Ashley!

Chapter 8

Mary-Kate and Ashley Today

On *Full House*, Michelle once got in trouble at school when she accidentally let the class bird out of its cage. But by the end of the episode, she made up for it by replacing the bird.

Real life, though, can be a little more complicated! Mary-Kate and Ashley's home life is probably a lot like yours. They sometimes have school problems, questions about boys, worries about their hair. And those kinds of problems are hardly ever solved as fast as they are on TV!

Like all kids, the girls have to listen to their parents. They have chores to do around the house. They have to take out the garbage and make their beds. They have to be in bed by a certain time every night. And they have to follow strict rules about eating junk food.

If they behave themselves and do their chores, Mary-Kate and Ashley earn an allowance of $10 a week. "We usually save that money up to buy cool stuff," says Mary-Kate.

But what happens if they break a rule? They might lose their allowance, and sometimes they're grounded.

Mary-Kate, Ashley, Trent, and Lizzie divide their time between their mom's house and their dad's house. Their parents are careful not to let Mary-Kate and Ashley's careers get in the way of having a normal family and social life. When they were younger, the girls were in a Brownies troop. Now Mary-Kate goes riding and they both attend cheerleading practice. In 1999, they were elected captains of their cheerleading squad for the homecoming game. The girls' parents encouraged them both to take up kickboxing.

Ashley and Mary-Kate have plenty of time to see their friends, as long as their homework gets done. It's very important Mary-Kate and Ashley keep up their grades, no matter how busy their careers get.

Like any students, though, the girls each have classes that aren't their favorites. Because they are both into language and communication, math tends to be their least favorite class. But they still work hard at doing the very best they can.

Luckily, Mary-Kate and Ashley are in a great school. No one makes a big deal about their being celebrities or being twins. "The only thing they give us a hard time about is being short," reveals Mary-Kate, with a grin. "We're *really* short," Ashley adds. "Our brother Trent says it takes two of us just to make one person." (When this book was written, Ashley was 4 feet 9 1/2 inches, and Mary-Kate was 4 feet 8 1/2 inches. But by the time you read this, they'll be taller!)

As the girls entered eighth grade, they switched schools. That can be pretty scary sometimes, even for Mary-Kate and Ashley. But the twins always try to look on the bright side. And they're usually willing to try anything.

The one thing that *does* make them nervous is performing in front of a live audience.

When they were seven, they spoke at Walt Disney World onstage in front of 3,000 kids and parents. They did a great job. But still they get nervous in front of live crowds. The girls don't have any problem at all making movies. If they need to film a scene over again, they do. It's all edited later and any mistakes the girls make get left out. But it's different when they appear on a talk show, like *The Rosie O'Donnell Show*. "You can't do it again if you mess up," says Mary-Kate. Through practice, though, the girls are getting over their fear of appearing live. "We do a lot of deep-breathing beforehand," says Mary-Kate. "That usually does it."

As they enter their teen years, the girls are finding new things to worry about. Like boys. Right now, Mary-Kate and Ashley are starting to attend boy-girl parties at school. But it probably won't be long before they're asking permission to go out on that first date!

What kind of guy would make a good boyfriend when the time is right? They both like independent boys who can think for themselves. "He has to be funny, cute, and nice. And he can't whine a lot," suggests Mary-Kate. Ashley adds that she likes boys who are "funny, and cute—and not clingy!"

As the girls get older, they're also starting to care more about makeup and clothes. "I like to look at *Vogue*," says Ashley. "Mary-Kate didn't used to care about fashion as much, but now she's getting more and more interested."

The girls love to choose their own clothes. Now that they're teenagers they want clothes that are sophisticated and trendy. But because they're small for their age, adult clothes are often too big on them. So Mary-Kate and Ashley either buy adult clothes and have them cut down—or they have clothes made specially for them.

"We love to look at designs and sample materials and pick out what we like," Ashley says. In fact, the girls have developed such good fashion sense that they've become trendsetters themselves.

"Sometimes we wear an outfit in the movies or on TV, and we see the same style in the stores six months later," Mary-Kate says. "It's fun to stay ahead of the trends."

These days, Mary-Kate and Ashley's favorite clothes are low-waisted pants and pencil skirts, worn with colorful tops and sweater sets. They like to wear lots of accessories—leather cuffs around their wrists, turquoise bracelets, little rope or beaded chokers, ankle bracelets, and all sorts of jewelry. "We like to wear stuff in our hair, too," says Mary-Kate, "like sparkle clips and beaded headbands." "And don't forget shoes," Ashley adds. "Especially platform sandals and thongs!"

At age 11, the girls discovered lip gloss. They love trying out different colors. Ashley also experiments with blushes and eye shadows. After years of watching professionals put on their makeup at work, Mary-Kate and Ashley have a pretty good idea how it's done.

Both girls will break out the makeup brushes if they have a special event to attend. Mary-Kate prefers more natural colors, like peaches and soft pinks. Ashley leans toward light pastels, mostly pinks and purples.

But both of them have learned that the trick to looking great is feeling great. And that comes from having a good diet and getting plenty of exercise. Mary-Kate and Ashley both stay active with kickboxing. And they eat lots of fruits, salad, and fish. The girls aren't really interested in candy anymore. Instead of soda, they'll usually reach for juice or water.

"I do have one big weakness," Mary-Kate admits. "It's gum. I'll stuff five pieces in my mouth if no one is looking!"

Mary-Kate and Ashley have hopes and dreams just like you. Some of Mary-Kate and Ashley's dreams are already coming true. But they know it can happen for *you*, too!

"If you really want to do something, go for it," advises Ashley. "Work hard and one day you can succeed!"

Chapter 9

What's Next?

1992

Mary-Kate: *"I want to be a candymaker and a cowgirl when I grow up."*

Ashley: *"I would like to be a candymaker and an actress. The food scenes are so much fun!"*

1994

Mary-Kate: *"I want to be an animal trainer for the movies. I want to have my own horse ranch."*

Ashley: *"I want to be a makeup artist, or I might keep acting."*

1997

Mary-Kate: *"I would like to train dolphins and whales, preferably at Sea World."*

Ashley: *"I really like acting. It's a lot of fun. And I*

would like to direct someday, too."

As they've grown up, Mary-Kate and Ashley's ideas about what they'd like to do in the future sure have changed (Ashley's plans always include acting, though). Now that the girls are teenagers, a whole new world of choices awaits them. So what will they do next?

Will they go to college after high school?

Continue to act?

Move to a career behind the camera?

How about all of the above?

It's certainly possible! Mary-Kate and Ashley have proven they are talented in show business *and* in school. There's no reason why they can't do it all!

Soon the girls will be deciding which college they want to attend—and if they'll be going together. Right now, Mary-Kate's biggest wish for a college is that it have a riding program. She doesn't want to be far from her horses! Ashley wants to make sure the school has a great dance and theater department.

For now, Mary-Kate and Ashley are looking very carefully at their next acting roles. The roles they want to play are a bit more grown-up.

The girls also want to branch out and play different kinds of characters. Like the witches on *Sabrina: The Teenage Witch* and *Charmed*, for example. "That would be fun," Ashley says. "We really want to do an action movie, too," adds Mary-Kate. "Car chases. Stunts. Danger."

One thing the girls may try someday is directing. Since they've grown up in front of a camera, they've learned the basics. When one of them is acting, the other is behind the scenes, looking through the camera lens or checking out the shot on a TV monitor. And the girls ask lots of questions.

Mary-Kate and Ashley actually take a very active role in producing now. They read scripts, ask for changes in them, make casting decisions, choose story ideas for movies, TV shows, videos, and interactive games, and meet frequently with their directors. "We love getting involved," Ashley explains. "It's a complete blast."

But for now, acting is still Ashley and Mary-Kate's number-one interest. They've always been given the chance to just be regular kids. "If the girls ever decide they've had enough, that's fine," says their mom. "But so far, that hasn't come close to happening."

"We would say `We've had enough,'" Mary-Kate says, "if we wanted to quit." She turns to her twin and they each break into a big grin. "But we're not going to say it because we love doing this," Ashley adds.

Mary-Kate & Ashley: Our Story

One thing is definitely in the future: Mary-Kate and Ashley Olsen are going to be having fun—*together!*

"Maybe when we're older we'll split up, but I doubt it," Mary-Kate says. "We're going to be doing all our movies together until we're at least sixteen!"

COOL MARY-KATE AND ASHLEY FUN FACTS!

• When *Full House* began, Mary-Kate's name was *not* hyphenated.

• In photographs where the girls are dressed in blue and pink or red, it's almost always Mary-Kate wearing blue and Ashley in pink or red.

• In 1992, the girls had a talking Michelle doll that looked just like them—and in 2000 they're each going to be fashion dolls for Mattel!

• Mary-Kate and Ashley rode on the Jell-O float in the 1997 Macy's Thanksgiving Day Parade.

• At age six, Mary-Kate and Ashley became the youngest producers in the history of Hollywood.

• The girls frequently use the same photographers—and they're twins, too!

• Mary-Kate and Ashley were named Teen Ambassadors to the U.S. Women's World Cup soccer team in 1999, the year the team won!

• The girls both like to fall asleep with their televisions on.

• Nickelodeon viewers voted them the Best Female Actresses of the Year for the film *It Takes Two* in 1996.

• They won this award again in 1998 for their roles

as Mary-Kate and Ashley Burke on *Two of a Kind*.
•The girls played themselves in an episode of the soap opera *All My Children*.
•Mary-Kate and Ashley have been featured in more than 40,000 newspaper stories throughout their careers, they have been on the cover of over a dozen magazines, and they have appeared nearly 100 times on TV talk shows.

MARY-KATE

FULL NAME: Mary-Kate Olsen (no middle name)
BIRTHDATE: June 13, 1986 (about two minutes after Ashley)
HAIR COLOR: Strawberry blond
EYE COLOR: Blue-green
FEATURES: Left-handed
One inch shorter than Ashley
A freckle on her right cheek
Rounder face
FAVORITE HOBBY: Horseback riding
FAVORITE CARD GAME: Spit
TO EARN HER ALLOWANCE: Feeds the dog, takes out the trash, cleans her room
FAVORITE STORES: Fred Segal and Planet Funk in Los Angeles and Annasui in New York

FAVORITE CLOTHING: Blue jeans, T-shirts, cashmere sweaters

FAVORITE TELEVISION SHOWS: *Friends* and *Whose Line Is it Anyway?*

FAVORITE MOVIE: *Titanic*

FAVORITE BOOKS: Adventure and mystery books

FAVORITE TITLE: *Oliver Twist* by Charles Dickens

CELEBRITY CRUSH: Brad Pitt

FAVORITE BOY BAND: 'N Sync

FAVORITE SCHOOL SUBJECT: Creative writing

LEAST FAVORITE SCHOOL SUBJECT: Math

AFTER-SCHOOL ACTIVITIES: Rollerblading, swimming, horseback riding, cheerleading

PICK A NUMBER: 8

FAVORITE THEME PARK: Disneyland

WHAT'S IN HER PURSE: Lip gloss, gum, wallet, and more lip gloss

FAVORITE SPORTS: Football and basketball

FAVORITE EXERCISE: Kickboxing

FAVORITE ANIMAL: Horse

COLLECTS: Candles and Beanie Babies

RISE AND SHINE: "I like to wake up early!"

DRINK OF CHOICE: Juice

FAVORITE FOOD: Pizza and tacos

FAVORITE VEGGIE: Broccoli

FAVORITE ICE CREAM: Mocha

FAVORITE GUM FLAVOR: Strawberry
FAVORITE COLORS: Maroon and blue
HOLIDAY OF CHOICE: Christmas
WISH LIST: A pet tiger
INSTRUMENT: Violin
IF SHE DOESN'T ACT IN THE FUTURE: "I'd like
to be a championship horse rider."

ASHLEY

FULL NAME: Ashley Fuller Olsen (Fuller is her
mom's maiden name)
BIRTHDATE: June 13, 1986 (about two minutes
before Mary-Kate)
HAIR COLOR: Strawberry blond
EYE COLOR: Blue-green
FEATURES: Right-handed
An inch taller than Mary-Kate
Has a freckle above her lip
Oval face
FAVORITE HOBBY: Dance (ballet, hip-hop, and
swing)
FAVORITE CARD GAME: Spit
TO EARN HER ALLOWANCE: Vacuums, takes out
the trash, cleans her room
FAVORITE STORES: Fred Segal and Miu Miu in Los

Angeles and Scoop and Irene Wong in New York
FAVORITE CLOTHING: Cashmere sweaters, bracelets, fun necklaces
FAVORITE TELEVISION SHOWS: *Party of Five* and *Friends*
FAVORITE MOVIE: *Ever After*
FAVORITE BOOKS: Mysteries and historical fiction
FAVORITE TITLE: *Of Mice and Men* by John Steinbeck
FAVORITE SCHOOL SUBJECT: English
LEAST FAVORITE SCHOOL SUBJECT: Math
AFTER-SCHOOL ACTIVITIES: Rollerblading, swimming, cheerleading, hanging with friends
PICK A NUMBER: 8
FAVORITE THEME PARK: Knott's Berry Farm
WHAT'S IN HER PURSE: Lip gloss, Kleenex, and gum
FAVORITE SPORT: Soccer
FAVORITE EXERCISE: Kickboxing
FAVORITE ANIMAL: Her dog, Lucy
COLLECTS: Teddy bears and Beanie Babies
RISE AND SHINE: "I like to sleep in!"
DRINK OF CHOICE: Juice
FAVORITE FOOD: Spaghetti
FAVORITE VEGGIE: Broccoli
FAVORITE ICE CREAM: Cookie Dough

FAVORITE GUM FLAVOR: Grape
FAVORITE COLORS: Yellow, purple, and blue
HOLIDAY OF CHOICE: Christmas
WISH LIST: "All the clothes I want!"
INSTRUMENT: "I used to play the piano."
IF SHE DOESN'T ACT IN THE FUTURE: "I'd like
   to be a dancer or a director."

MARK YOUR CALENDAR:
Mary-Kate and Ashley's birthday: June 13, 1986

YOU ASKED! THEY ANSWERED!

Dear Mary-Kate and Ashley,
Your videos are great! My favorite is _Shark_
Encounter. What do you like to do in the summer?
Do you go to the beach? If you do, watch out for
the sharks!

> **Sara**
> **Williamsville, NY**

Dear Sara,
We spend lots of summers making movies and
videos. But we love going to the beach too! And
we've never seen a shark (except at Sea World).

> Ashley

Dear Mary-Kate and Ashley,
What do you do when you get bored?

> **Shantel**
> **Anacortes, WA**

Dear Shantel,
When I'm bored, my favorite thing to do is watch an
old movie on TV. But when she's bored, Ashley goes
shopping!

> Mary-Kate

Dear Mary-Kate and Ashley,
It Takes Two **was the best! Do you like to be in the movies?**

> **Tanja**
> **Anacortes, WA**

Dear Tanja,
We love making movies and videos. We have lots of fun and we meet the coolest people.

> Ashley

Dear Mary-Kate and Ashley,
My sisters and I are big fans of yours. Do you really travel around the world?

> **Hang, Hanh, Linda, & Juile**
> **Warren, MI**

Dear Hang, Hanh, Linda, & Juile,
We've traveled to really great places to make our movies and videos: Alaska, Hawaii, Florida, Canada, Paris, and lots of others. And this year we're going to Russia!

> Ashley

Dear Mary-Kate and Ashley,
You guys are so funny and pretty. What do your rooms look like?

> Brittany
> Riverside, CA

Dear Brittany,
We each have big, sunny rooms with white furniture and lots of pictures of friends on the walls.

> Mary-Kate

Dear Mary-Kate and Ashley,
We are sisters, too. We like having someone to play with so we are not lonely. What do you think is so special about being sisters?

> Katie and Olivia
> New York, NY

Dear Katie and Olivia,
We love being sisters because we know we can always go to each other for help and advice and friendship. We're *always* there for each other. Plus, we have a lot of fun!

> Mary-Kate and Ashley

THE MARY-KATE & ASHLEY COLLECTION

If you owned every book, video, interactive game, and recording Mary-Kate and Ashley have ever done, you'd need your own library to store everything! Here's a great way to keep track of what you have (and what you still need to collect!).

THE VIDEOS

☐ **Our First Video (1993)**
☐ **Our Music Video (1997)**

The Adventures of Mary-Kate & Ashley

☐ **The Case Of The Logical i Ranch (1994)**
☐ **The Case Of Thorn Mansion (1994)**
☐ **The Case Of The Mystery Cruise (1995)**
☐ **The Case Of The Fun House Mystery (1995)**
☐ **The Case Of The Christmas Caper (1995)**
☐ **The Case Of The Sea World Adventure (1996)**
☐ **The Case Of The U.S. Space Camp Mission (1996)**
☐ **The Case Of The Shark Encounter (1996)**
☐ **The Case Of The Hotel Who-Done-It (1996)**
☐ **The Case Of The Volcano Mystery (1997)**
☐ **The Case Of The U.S. Navy Adventure (1997)**

You're Invited to Mary-Kate & Ashley's

☐ **Sleepover Party (1995)**

☐ Hawaiian Beach Party (1996)
☐ Birthday Party (1997)
☐ Christmas Party (1997)
☐ Ballet Party (1998)
☐ Camp Out Party (1998)
☐ Mall Party (1998)
☐ Costume Party (1998)
☐ Fashion Party (1999)
☐ School Dance Party (2000)

THE MOVIES

☐ To Grandmother's House We Go (1992)
☐ Double, Double, Toil and Trouble (1993)
☐ How the West Was Fun (1994)
☐ It Takes Two (1995)
☐ Billboard Dad (1999)
☐ Passport to Paris (1999)
☐ Switching Goals (1999)

CASSETTES AND CDs

☐ Brother for Sale (1992)
☐ I Am the Cute One (1993)
☐ Give Us a Mystery (1994)
☐ Sleepover Party (1997)
☐ Birthday Party (1998)
☐ Ballet Party (1998)
☐ Mary-Kate and Ashley's Greatest Hits (2000)

INTERACTIVE GAMES

☐ Mary-Kate & Ashley's Dance Party of the Century–CD-ROM (2000)

☐ The New Adventures of Mary-Kate & Ashley–Game Boy Color (2000)

THE BOOKS

You're Invited to Mary-Kate & Ashley's

☐ Sleepover Party (1996)

☐ Hawaiian Beach Party (1996)

☐ Christmas Party (1997)

☐ Birthday Party (1998)

☐ Ballet Party (1998)

The Adventures of Mary-Kate & Ashley

☐ The Case Of The Sea World Adventure (1996)

☐ The Case Of The Mystery Cruise (1996)

☐ The Case Of The Fun House Mystery (1996)

☐ The Case Of The Christmas Caper (1996)

☐ The Case Of The U.S. Space Camp Mission (1996)

☐ The Case Of The Shark Encounter (1996)

☐ The Case Of The Hotel Who-Done-It (1997)

☐ The Case Of The Volcano Mystery (1997)

☐ The Case Of The U.S. Navy Adventure (1997)

☐ The Case Of Thorn Mansion (1997)

The New Adventures of Mary-Kate & Ashley

☐ The Case Of The Ballet Bandit (1998)

- ☐ The Case Of The 202 Clues (1998)
- ☐ The Case Of The Blue Ribbon Horse (1998)
- ☐ The Case Of The Haunted Camp (1998)
- ☐ The Case Of The Wild Wolf River (1998)
- ☐ The Case Of The Rock & Roll Mystery (1998)
- ☐ The Case Of The Missing Mummy (1998)
- ☐ The Case Of The Surprise Call (1999)
- ☐ The Case Of The Disappearing Princess (1999)
- ☐ The Case Of The Great Elephant Escape (1999)
- ☐ The Case Of The Summer Camp Caper (1999)
- ☐ The Case Of The Surfing Secret (1999)
- ☐ The Case Of The Green Ghost (1999)
- ☐ The Case Of The Big Scare Mountain Mystery (1999)
- ☐ The Case Of The Slam Dunk Mystery (2000)

Full House: Michelle

- ☐ The Great Pet Project (1995)
- ☐ The Super-Duper Sleepover Party (1995)
- ☐ My Two Best Friends (1997)
- ☐ Lucky, Lucky Day (1995)
- ☐ The Ghost in My Closet (1995)
- ☐ Ballet Surprises (1996)
- ☐ Major League Trouble (1996)
- ☐ My Fourth-Grade Mess (1996)
- ☐ Bunk 3, Teddy and Me (1996)
- ☐ My Best Friend Is a Movie Star (1996)
- ☐ The Big Turkey Escape (1996)
- ☐ The Substitute Teacher (1997)

☐ Calling All Planets (1997)
☐ I've Got a Secret (1997)
☐ How to Be Cool (1997)
☐ The Not-So-Great-Outdoors (1997)
☐ My Ho-Ho Horrible Christmas (1997)
☐ My Awesome Holiday Friendship Book (1997)
☐ My Almost Perfect Plan (1998)
☐ April Fools (1998)
☐ My Life Is a Three-Ring Circus (1998)
☐ Welcome to My Zoo (1998)
☐ The Problem with Pen-Pals (1998)
☐ Merry Christmas World! (1998)
☐ Tap Dance Trouble (1999)
☐ The Fastest Turtle in the West (1999)
☐ My Super Sleepover Party (1999)
☐ The Baby-sitting Boss (1999)
☐ The Wish I Wish I Never Wished (1999)
☐ Pigs, Pies and Plenty of Problems (1999)
☐ If I Were President (1999)
☐ How to Meet a Superstar (1999)

Full House: Sisters
☐ Two on the Town (1998)
☐ One Boss Too Many (1998)
☐ And the Winner Is . . . (1999)
☐ How to Hide a Horse (1999)
☐ Problems in Paradise (1999)

Two of a Kind

☐ It's a Twin Thing (1999)

☐ How to Flunk Your First Date (1999)

☐ The Sleepover Secret (1999)

☐ One Twin Too Many (1999)

☐ To Snoop or Not to Snoop (1999)

☐ My Sister the Supermodel (1999)

☐ Two's A Crowd (1999)

☐ Let's Party (1999)

☐ Calling All Boys (2000)

☐ Winner Take All (2000)

Other Titles

☐ My Mary-Kate & Ashley Mood Diary (1999)

☐ Mary-Kate & Ashley Be My Valentine (2000)

☐ It Takes Two Jr. Novelization Book (1995)

☐ It Takes Two Storybook (1995)

☐ Once Upon a Time with Mary-Kate & Ashley (1998)

☐ Mary-Kate & Ashley's Walt Disney World Adventure (1998)

☐ The New Adventures of Mary-Kate & Ashley: The Detective Kit (1998)

☐ Switching Goals (1999)

☐ Billboard Dad (1999)

☐ Mary-Kate and Ashley's Passport to Paris Scrapbook (2000)

CONTACT MARY-KATE AND ASHLEY!

Fans have found ways to get letters to Mary-Kate and Ashley. No matter where the mail is sent, it always seems to find its way to them (it just might take awhile!).

Because the girls have been in show business for so long, they've had several addresses. Here is the most up-to-date way to reach them. So grab a pencil and your address book!

But be warned: You may not hear back from the girls right away.

They're lucky enough to get thousands of letters every month from fans like you. Unfortunately, that's too many for them to respond to personally. Can you imagine if they did? The girls would have to write at least 150 letters every day—that's 75 each! They would never have time to go to school, go to work, or even sleep!

But Mary-Kate and Ashley love to hear from you. They especially appreciate your photos and drawings. "Having you out there and knowing you care really helps us when we're traveling so much," says Ashley.

"We love getting your cards and letters," adds Mary-Kate. "Thanks, you're the greatest!"

Joining Mary-Kate + Ashley's Fun Club is a great way to keep up with the busy girls. You'll receive cool pics and a great newsletter. It's just like getting your own letter back from Mary-Kate and Ashley!

LETTERS TO MARY-KATE & ASHLEY

Mary-Kate + Ashley's Fun Club™
c/o Dualstar Entertainment Group, Inc.
859 Hollywood Way, Suite 325
Burbank, CA 91505

Their Official Web Site!

ABOUT THE AUTHOR

Damon Romine is an entertainment journalist. He has co-authored a series of Life Stories books on the Backstreet Boys, 'N Sync, Ricky Martin, Leonardo DiCaprio, Matt Damon, the Spice Girls, and *Dawson's Creek*. Damon is currently the West Coast Editor of the teen magazine *J-14*. He lives in Los Angeles with his beagle, Abby.

Take a Peek Inside our Diaries!

3 Very Special Books in the Two of a Kind Series

Dear Diary,

When Mary-Kate and I packed up to come to White Oak Academy, I thought boarding school would be like regular school. But it's totally strange! The principal is called a head-mistress, seventh grade is called first form, and my roommate is called - well, I call her weird. And the worst thing is, there's this huge dance coming up.

I know, I know. I, Ashley Burke, don't want to go to a dance? But here's the deal - the girls have to ask the boys. And I don't know any!

- Ashley

OUT NOW!

–look for *Winner Take All* coming in April 2000 and –P.S. *Wish You Were Here* coming in June 2000

ALL-NEW STORIES, SETTINGS, AND DIARY FORMAT–SAME AWESOME SERIES!

www.maryandashley.com

IT'S YOUR FIRST CLASS TICKET TO ADVENTURE!

Own it only on Video!

Mary-Kate   **Ashley**

Take a peek at the new Hottest Fashion Dolls!

Coming your way Spring 2000!

www.marykateandashley.com   www.barbie.com

Each sold separately.

DUALSTAR
ENTERTAINMENT
GROUP

GAME GIRLS

SOLVE ANY CRIME BY DINNER TIME™

The New Adventures of
MARY-KATE & ASHLEY™

GAME BOY COLOR

PARTY DOWN WITH THE HOTTEST DANCES AND COOLEST FASHIONS

MARY-KATE & ASHLEY'S
DANCE PARTY OF THE CENTURY™

PC
CD-ROM

www.marykateandashley.com

DUALSTAR
INTERACTIVE

www.acclaim.net